I0415093

Individualist Anarchism:
The Selected Works of Emile Armand

Individualist Anarchism: The Selected Works of Emile Armand

SAI Press
Dickinson, ND

This edition first published July, 2021.

ISBN: 978-1-257-63140-7

Contents

Is the Illegalist Anarchist our Comrade?

When we consider the thief as such we can't say that we find him less human than other classes of society. The members of the great criminal gangs have mutual relations that are strongly marked with communism. If they represent a survival from a prior age, we can also consider them as the precursors of a better age in the future. In all cities they know where to address themselves so they'll be received and hidden. Up to a certain point they show themselves to be generous and prodigal towards those of their milieu. If they consider the rich as their natural enemies, as a legitimate prey – a point of view quite difficult to contradict – a large number of them are animated by the sprit of Robin Hood; when it comes to the poor many thieves show themselves to have a good heart.

(Edward Carpenter: *Civilization, its Cause and Cure*.)

I am not an enthusiast of illegalism. I am an *alegal*. Illegalism is a dangerous last resort for he who engages in it, even temporarily, a last resort that should neither be preached nor advocated. But the question I propose to study is not that of asking whether or not an illegal trade is perilous or not, but if the anarchist who earns his daily bread by resorting to trades condemned by the police and tribunals is right or wrong to expect that an anarchist who accepts working for a boss treat him as a comrade, a comrade whose point of view we defend in broad daylight and who we don't deny when he falls into the grips of the police or the decisions of judges. (Unless he asks us to remain silent about his case)

The illegalist anarchist in fact doesn't want us to treat him like a "poor relation" who we don't dare publicly admit to because this would do harm to the anarchist cause, or because not separating ourselves from him when the representatives of capitalist vengeance come crushing down on him would risk losing the sympathy of syndicalists and the clientele of petit-bourgeois anarchist sympathizers for the anarchist movement.

It is by design that the illegalist anarchist addresses himself to his comrade who is exploited by a boss, that is, *who feels himself* to be exploited. He hardly expects to be understood by those who work at a job that is to their taste. Among these latter he places the anarchist doctrinaires and propagandists who spread, defend, and expose ideas in accordance their opinions – this is what we hope, at least. Even if they only receive a pitiful , a very pitiful salary for their labor, their moral situation isn't comparable to the position of an anarchist working under the surveillance of a foreman and obliged to suffer all day the promiscuity of people whose company is antagonistic to him. This is why the illegalist anarchist denies to those who have jobs that please them the right to cast judgment on his profession on the margins of the law.

All those who do written or spoken propaganda work that is to their taste, all those who work at a profession they like, too often forget that they are privileged in comparison with the mass of the others, their comrades, those who are forced to put on their harness every morning, from January first to the next New Year's Eve and work at tasks for which they have no liking.[1]

The illegalist anarchist claims he is every bit as much a comrade as the merchant, the secretary at town hall, or the dancing master, none of whom in any way modify – and certainly to no greater degree than he – the economic conditions of current society. A lawyer, a doctor, a teacher can send articles to an anarchist newspaper and give talks at tiny libertarian circles all they want, they nevertheless remain both the supporters and the supported of the *archist* system, which gave them the monopoly that permits them to exercise their profession and the regulations they are obliged to submit to if they want to continue working at their trades.

It is not an exaggeration to say that any anarchist who accepts being exploited for the profit of a private boss or the state-boss is committing an act of treason towards anarchist ideas. He is, in effect, reinforcing domination and exploitation, is contributing to maintaining the existence of *archism*. It is doubtless true that becoming aware of his inconsistency he strives to redeem or repair his conduct by making propaganda. But whatever the propaganda done by the exploited he still remains an accomplice of the exploiters, a cooperator in the system of exploitation that rules the conditions under which production takes place.

This is why it is not exact to say that the anarchist "who works," who submits to the system of domination and exploitation in place, is a victim. He is an accomplice as much as he is a victim. All of the exploited, legal or illegal, cooperate in the state of domination. There is no difference between the anarchist worker who earned 175,000 or 200,000 francs in thirty years of labor and who , with his savings, has purchased a hut in the country, and the illegalist anarchist who grabs a safe containing 200,000 francs and with this sum acquires a house by the seaside. Both are anarchists in word only, it is true, but the difference between them is that the anarchist worker submits to the terms of the economic contract that the leaders of the social milieu impose on him, while the anarchist thief *does not submit to them.*

The law protects the exploited as much

as the exploiter, the dominated as much as the dominator in their mutual social relations, and as long as he submits the anarchist is as well protected in his property and his person as the *archist*. The law makes no distinction between the *archist* and the anarchist as long as both accept the injunctions of the social contract. Whether they will or no, the anarchists who submit: bosses, workers, employees, functionaries, have the public forces, tribunals, social conventions, and official educators on their side. This is the reward for their submission: when they constrain – by moral persuasion or the force of the law – the *archist* employer to pay his anarchist employee, the forces of social preservation could care less that deep down, or even on the outside, the wage earner is hostile to the wage system.

On the contrary, the opponent of, the

rebel against the social contract, the illegal anarchist has against him *the entire social organization* when in order to "live his life" he leaps over all intermediary stages in order immediately reach the goal that the submissive anarchist will reach only later, if ever. He runs an enormous risk, and it is only fair that this risk be compensated for by immediate results, if there are results at all.

The recourse to ruse, which the illegalist anarchist constantly practices, is a procedure employed by all revolutionaries. Secret societies are an aspect of this. In order to put up subversive posters we wait for policemen to walk in another sector. An anarchist who leaves for America conceals his moral, political and philosophical point of view. Whatever he might be, apparently submissive or openly rebellious, the anarchist is always an illegal as regards the law. When he propagates his anarchist ideas he contravenes the special laws that repress anarchist propaganda; even more, by his anarchist mentality he opposes himself to the written law itself in its essence, for the law is the concretion of archaism.[2]

The rebellious anarchist cannot fail to be found sympathetic by the submissive anarchist who feels himself to be submissive. In his illegal attitude the anarchist who either couldn't or wouldn't break with legality recognizes himself, realized logically. The temperament, the reflections of the submissive anarchist can lead him to disapprove certain acts of the rebellious anarchist, but can never render him personally antipathetic.[3]

The illegalist answers the revolutionary anarchist who reproaches him with immediately seeking his financial well being by saying that he, the revolutionary, does nothing different. The economic revolutionary expects from the revolution an improvement in his personal economic situation: if not he wouldn't be a revolutionary. The revolution will give him what he hoped for or it won't, just as an illegal operation furnishes or doesn't furnish what was counted on to he who executes it.. It's simply a question of dates. Even when the economic question is not a factor one only makes a revolution if one expects a personal benefit, a religious, political, intellectual or perhaps ethical benefit. Every revolutionary is an egoist.

*

Does the explanation of acts of "expropriation" committed by illegalists have an unfavorable influence, in general and in particular, on anarchist propaganda?

In order to answer this question, which is the most important of all questions, one must not lose sight for a single second of the fact that in coming into the world, or in penetrating any country, the human unit finds economic conditions that are imposed on it. Whatever one's opinions, one must, in order to live (or die) in peace, submit to constraint. Where there is constraint the contract is no longer valid, since it is unilateral, and bourgeois codes themselves that a commitment subscribed to under threat is of no legal value. The anarchist thus finds himself in a state of legitimate defense against the executors and the partisans of the imposed economic contract. For example, we have never heard an anarchist, exercising an illegal trade, call for a society based on universal banditry. His situation, his acts, are solely in relation to the economic contract that the capitalists or the unilaterals impose even on those revolted by its clauses. The illegalism of anarchists is only transitory: a last resort.

If the social milieu granted anarchists the inalienable possession of their personal means of production; if they could freely, and without any fiscal restriction (taxes, customs duties) , dispose of their products; if they allowed to be employed among them an exchange value that would be struck with no tax, all of this at their own risk, illegalism, in my sense of the word (i.e., economic illegalism), would no longer be understood. Economic illegalism is thus purely accidental.[4]

In any event, economic or otherwise, illegalism is a function of legalism. The day authority disappears – political, intellectual and economic authority – the illegalists will also disappear.

It is on this path that we must orient ourselves in order for illegalist acts to benefit anarchist propaganda.

Every anarchist, submissive or not, considers as a comrade he among his like who refuses to accept military servitude. It is inexplicable then why his attitude would change when it's a matter of refusing to serve economically.

We can easily understand that anarchists don't want to contribute to the economic life of a country that doesn't accord them the possibility of explaining by the pen or the spoken word and that limits their faculties and their possibilities of realization and association, in whatever realm. At the same time they, for their part, would allow non-anarchists to conduct themselves however they wish. Those anarchists who agree to participate in the economic functioning of societies where they cannot live according to their desires are inconsistent. We can't understand why they object to those who rebel against this state of things.

The rebel against economic servitude finds himself, *from the instinct for preservation,* by the need and the will to life, to appropriate the production of others. This instinct is not only primordial, it is legitimate, the illegalists affirm, compared to capitalist accumulation, accumulation which the capitalist, taken personally, does not need to exist, accumulation which is a superfluity. Now who are these "others" who the reasoning illegalist attacks – the anarchist who exercises an illegal profession. The "others" are those who want majorities to dominate or oppress minorities, they are the partisan of the domination or the dictatorship of one class or caste over others, they are the voters, the supporters of the state, of the monopolies and privileges it implies. In reality, these "others" are an enemy for the anarchist, irreconcilable adversaries. The moment he economically lays into him, the illegalist anarchist no longer sees in him, cannot see in him, anything but an instrument of the *archist* system.

These explanations provided we can't say that the illegalist anarchist is wrong who considers himself betrayed when those anarchists who preferred following less perilous roads than his abandon or don't care to explain their attitudes.

I repeat what I said when I began these lines; since there is a last resort, that offered by illegalism is the most dangerous of all, and it must be demonstrated that it brings in more than it costs, which is something quite exceptional. The illegalist anarchist who is thrown in prison has no favors to hope for as far as probation or reduction of his sentence. As the saying goes, his dossier is marked in red. But with this caveat, it must still be pointed out that in order to be seriously practiced illegalism demands a strongly tempered temperament, a sureness of oneself that doesn't belong to everyone. As with all experiences in anarchist life that don't march in step with the routines of daily existence, it is to be feared that the practices of illegalist anarchism take over the will and the thought of the illegalist to such an extent that it renders him incapable of any other activity, any other attitude. The same also goes for certain legal trades that spare those who practice it the need to be at a factory or an office.

CONCLUSIONS

Economic anarchists and economic leaders and rulers *impose* on workers working conditions incompatible with the anarchist notion of life, i.e., with the absence of exploitation of man by man. In principle an anarchist refuses to allow to have working conditions imposed on him or to allow himself to be exploited. He only accepts on condition of abdicating and submitting.

And there is no difference between submitting to pay taxes, submitting to exploitation, and submitting to military service.

It is understood that the majority of

anarchists submit. "We obtain more from legality by rusing with it, by fooling it, than by confronting it face to face." This is true. But the anarchist who ruses with the law has no reason to brag about it. In doing this he escapes the dangerous consequences of insubordination, the penal colony , the "most abject of slaveries." But if he doesn't have to suffer all this, the submissive anarchist has to deal with "professional deformation": by externally conforming to the law a number of anarchists finish by no longer reacting at all and pass to the other side of the barricades. An exceptional temperament is necessary in order to ruse with the law without allowing oneself to be caught up in the net of legality.

As for the anarchist-producer in the current economic milieu: this is a myth. Where are the anarchists who produce anti-authoritarian values? By their productivity almost all anarchists collaborate in maintaining the current economic state of affairs. You'll never make me believe that the anarchist who builds prisons, barracks, churches; who manufactures arms, munitions, uniforms; who prints codes, political journals, religious books, who stocks them, transports them, sells them, is participating in anti-authoritarian production. Even the anarchist who produces necessary items for the use of voters and the elected is false to his convictions.

It is not up to either verbal propagandists or men of the pen to accuse obscure individualists of materially benefiting from their ideas. Do they count as nothing the "moral" and sometimes pecuniary benefit their efforts procure for them? Renown spreads their names "from one end of the earth to the other;" they have disciples, translators, slanderers, persecutors. For what do they count all this?

I find it only fair that every labor receive a salary, in all domains. It is fair that if you suffer for your opinions you should also profit from them. What matters is that by violence, trickery, ruse, theft, fraud or imposition of any kind this profit not be realized to the detriment or harm or wrong of one's comrades, of those from "our world."

In the current social milieu anarchism extends from Tolstoy to Bonnot: Warren, Proudhon, Kropotkin, Ravachol, Caserio, Louise Michel, Libertad, Pierre Chardon, Tchorny, the tendencies they represent or that are represented by certain living animators or inspirations whose names are of little importance, are like the nuances of a rainbow where each individual chooses the tint that most pleases his vision.

In placing oneself from the strictly individualist anarchist point of view – and it is with this that I will conclude – the criterion for camaraderie doesn't reside in the fact that tone is an office worker, factory worker, functionary, newspaper seller, smuggler or thief, it resides in this, that legal or illegal, MY comrade will in the first place seek to sculpt his own individuality, to spread anti-authoritarian ideas wherever he can, and finally, by rendering life among those who share his ideas as agreeable as possible will reduce to as useless and avoidable suffering to as negligible a quantity as possible.

Notes

1. One day in Brussels I discussed the question with Elisée Reclus. He said, in conclusion: "I work at something that pleases me; I don't see where I have the right to judge those who don't want to work at something that doesn't please them."

2. Though I don't have the statistics required, a reading of anarchist newspapers indicates that the number of those justly or unjustly condemned – to prison, penal colonies, or gunned down – for revolutionary anarchist agitation (including "propaganda by the deed") is far greater than those justly or unjustly condemned, or gunned down, for illegalism. The theoreticians of revolutionary anarchism bear a large part of responsibility for these condemnations, for they have never couched the propaganda in favor of revolutionary acts with the same reserves that the serious "explainers" of the illegalist act oppose to the practice of illegalism.

3. The anarchist whose illegalism attacks the state or known exploiters has never indisposed "the worker" concerning anarchism. I was in Amiens during the trial of Jacob, who often

attacked colonial officers. Thanks to the explanations in "Germinal" the workers of Amiens were quite sympathetic to Jacob and the ideas of individual expropriation. Even non-anarchist, the illegal who attacks a banker, a factory owner, a manufacturer, a treasurer, a postal wagon, etc, is found sympathetic by the exploited, who consider as valets or squealers those wage earners who defend the coin or the cash of their boss, private or state. I have noted this hundreds of times.

4. Socially speaking, the day when the costs for the keeping of a property will be superior to what it brings in property, daughter of exploitation, will disappear.

What is an Anarchist?

A chaos of beings, of acts and ideas; a disordered, bitter, merciless struggle; a perpetual lie, a blindly spinning wheel, one day placing someone at the pinnacle, and the next day crushing him: these are just a few of the images that depict current society, if it were possible for it to be depicted. The brush of the greatest of painters and the pen of the greatest of writers would splinter like glass if we were to employ them to express even a distant echo of the tumult and melee that the is depicted by the clash of appetites, aspirations, hatreds and devotions that collide and mix together the different categories among which men are parceled out.

Who will ever precisely express the unfinished battle between private interests and collective needs? The sentiments of individuals and the logic of generalities? All of this makes up current society, and none of this suffices to describe it. A minority which possesses the faculty to produce and consume and the possibility to parasitically exist in a thousand different forms: fixed and movable property, capital as tools or as funds, capital as teaching and capital as education.

Facing it an immense majority, which possesses nothing but its arms or brains or other productive organs which it is forced to rent, lease, or prostitute, not only in order to procure what it needs so as not to die of hunger, but also to permit a small number of holders of the power or property or exchange values to live more or less in luxury at its expense. A mass, rich and poor, slaves of immemorial, hereditary prejudices, some because this is in their interest, the others because they are sunk in ignorance or don't want to escape it. A multitude whose cult is that of money and the prototype of the rich man, the rule of the mediocre incapable of both great vices and great virtues. And the mass of degenerates on high and down low, without profound aspirations, without any other goal than that of arriving at a position of enjoyment and ease, even if it means crushing, if necessary, the friends of yesterday, become the downtrodden of today.

A provisional state that ceaselessly threatens to transform itself into a definitive one, and a definitive state that threatens to never be anything but provisional. Lives that give the lie to espoused convictions, and convictions that serve as a springboard for crooked ambitions.

Free thinkers who show themselves to be more clericalist than the clerical, and believers who show themselves to be coarse materialists. The superficial individual who wants pass for profound and the profound individual who doesn't succeed in being taken seriously. No one would deny that this is a portrait of society, and no thinking person would fail to see that this painting does not even begin to depict reality. Why? Because there is a mask placed before every face; because no one a care to *be*, because all aspire only to seem. To seem: this is the supreme ideal, and if we so avidly desire ease and wealth, it is in order to seem, since only money now allows one to make an impression.

This mania, this passion, this race for appearances, for what can procure them, devours both the rich man and the vagabond, the most erudite and the illiterate. The worker who curses his foreman wishes to become one in turn; the merchant who evaluates his commercial honor to be of an unequalled price doesn't hesitate to carry out dishonorable deals; the small shop owner, member of patriotic and nationalist electoral committees, hastens to transmit his orders to foreign manufacturers as soon as he finds this profitable. The socialist lawyer, advocate of the poverty-stricken proletariat herded into the malodorous parts of the city, passes his vacations in a chateau or resides in the wealthy neighborhoods of the city, where fresh air is abundant. The free thinker still willingly marries in church, and often has his children baptized there. The religious man doesn't dare express his ideas, since ridiculing religion is the done thing. Where is sincerity to be found? The gangrene has spread everywhere. We find it in the family, where often father, mother, and children hate and deceive each other while saying that they love each other, while leading each other to believe that they feel affection for each other. We see it at work in the couple, where the husband and wife not meant for each other betray each other, not daring to break the ties that bind them. It is there for all to see in groups, where each seeks to supplant his neighbor in the esteem of the president, the secretary, or the treasurer, while waiting to assume their place when they no longer need them. It abounds in the acts of devotion, in public doings, in private conversations, in official harangues. To seem! To seem! To seem pure, disinterested, and generous, while at the same time we consider purity, disinterest, and generosity as vain foolishness; to seem moral, honest, and virtuous when probity, virtue, and morality are the least concerns of those who profess them.

Where can one find a person who escapes corruption, who consents not to seem?

We don't claim to ever have met such a one. We note that sincere, eminently sincere individuals are rare. We affirm that the number of human beings who work disinterestedly is quite limited. Right or wrong, I have more respect for the individual who cynically admits to wanting to enjoy life by profiting from others than for the liberal and philanthropic bourgeois whose lips resound with grandiose words, but whose fortune is built on the concealed exploitation of the unfortunate.

It will be objected that we are allowing ourselves to be led by our indignation. That in the first place nothing proves that our anger and invectives are not also a way of seeming. Be aware: what you will find here are observations, opinions, theses: it will be left to the reader to determine what they are worth. The pages that follow are not marked with the seal of infallibility. We don't seek to convert anyone to our point of view. Our goal is to make those who browse these pages reflect, with the right to accept or reject that which is not in accord with their own convictions.

It will be objected that this is dealing with the question at too high a level, or from a metaphysical point of view; that we must descend to the level of concrete reality. The reality is this: that current society is the result of a long historical process, perhaps still just beginning; that humanity – or the different humanities – are simply at the point of seeking or preparing their way, that they are groping and stumbling; that they lose their way, find it again, advance, retreat, lose their way; that they are at times shaken to their foundation by certain crises, dragged along, cast on destiny's road and then slow down or march in place; that by scratching the polish, the varnish the surface of contemporary civilizations we would lay bare the stammering, the childishness, and the superstitions of the prehistoric. Who denies this? We accept that all these things render the "human problem" singularly complex.

Finally, it will be objected that it is folly to seek to discover, to establish the responsibility of the individual; that he is submerged, absorbed in his environment; that his ideas reflect the ideas and his acts the acts of those around him; that it can't be otherwise, and if from top to bottom of the social ladder it is "seeming" and not "being" that is the aspiration, the fault is that of the current stage of general evolution and not of the individual, the member of society, minuscule atom lost in a formidable aggregate.

We answer honestly that we don't intend to write for all the beings who make up society. Let us be understood: we address ourselves to those who think or are in the process of thinking, to those who have grown impatient from waiting for the mass, who can't or won't think; to those who can't adapt to appearances and who the current stage of society doesn't satisfy. We write for the curious, for thinkers, for the critical – for those who aren't content with formulas or empty solutions.

It's either the one or the other: either there's nothing else to be done than to allow the inevitable evolution to run its course, to cowardly bow before circumstances, to passively witness the parade of events and admit that, while waiting for something better, all is for the best in the best of societies. Our theses and opinions will not interest those who share this way of seeing things. Alternatively, without arming yourself with an exaggerated optimism, you can step off the main roads, withdraw to a great height, question yourself, look into yourself for the roots of our own malaise. We address ourselves to those not satisfied with the current society, to those who are thirsty for real life, for real activity and find only the artificial and the unreal around them. There are those who are thirsty for harmony and ask themselves why disorder and fratricidal struggles abound around them...

Let us conclude: the sprit that reflects and attentively considers men and things encounters in the complex of things we call society a nearly insurmountable barrier to truly free, independent, individual life. This is enough for him to qualify it as evil, and for him to wish for its disappearance.

The Individual and Dictatorship

We know that the State can perpetuate everything it wants to, because it has behind itself the armed force. The Soviet-state doesn't in the least differentiate itself in this respect from the Fascist one, or from any other powerful dictatorial State. The differentiation lies only in the interests that they represent. Any kind of forceful dictatorship, any sort of a stringent built-up State can , when it wants to, attain the same results as Fascism and Bolshevism. It only needs to have sufficient power in its hands and create an appropriate atmosphere, in order to be enabled to suppress oppositional interests and strangle the protests of those who disagree with it.

In the development-history of human beings since the world war, there has taken place a great change, a complete upturn. Four years, four terrible continuous years the rulers had no consideration, have not at all had any consideration with the social unity – the individual. They didn't see in the human being anything else than dead material, stockades who were not able to move themselves without "marching routes" and military orders. A few people set in a central bureau and pushed the masses hither and thither as it suited them best, or as it was demanded by the interests that they represented. One had to obey, without a murmur, without a thought, not asking as to the purpose. This condition has left such deep traces in the average thinking, that one must ask himself as to whether it is not needed to divide the history in two periods; the period before and the period after the war.

Military dictatorships, political dictatorships financial dictatorships, social and moral dictatorships – for all this heap of sufferings and evils that spread themselves over the world, we have to thank the war. In Russia, for instance, the stabilizing of production and consumption is simply being decreed, not mattering as to whether it suits to the producer or consumer or not. In Italy, decrees are issued that force one to be "virtuous" and so on..

Where then remains the individual, the person, the "I," the social unity?

I know what will be answered to me on this. I know already the arguments of the Stalins, the Mussolini's and all of that kind."

The State-citizen, subordinate, the administrative subject yes, but what then does he want? We are doing for him, for his well-being and security a great mass of things. Yes, we even make of him an atheist – or a religious person; we make, that his mind should work in the direction of communism – or fascism (just as it has been before proscribed to belong to an existing state religion); we make out of him a tiny wheel of the great mechanical mass production, as well as of the state mechanism-according to the demands of our interests. As a reciprocity for this mountain of deeds and good wills, that we do for him, we only ask a very small considerate thing, and this is; to renounce his personality and completely give himself over into our hands."

Herein lies the problem; does it pay to surrender our personality into the hands of dictators – for the "beneficial deeds" of a force-dictatorship with drums and trays and with flying flags?

If we were animals, herded together in a stockade, then the eating part would be the only real thing that would interest us, and it would not be so important as to whether the trough is colored Bolshevik-red or Fascist-black (taking it for granted that there is at all a trough), whether the food-distributor carries upon his cap a soviet-star or a fascist insignia or a swastika, the main thing would be the eating part.

But when one doesn't consider oneself as a stockade-animal, when one doesn't place the eating above one's determined, self-acknowledged, ever-developing personality and its traits, then the entire program changes.

There arise then different questions. For

instance, as to whether the forced stabilizing of the production and of the consumption is as beneficial for the formation of this personality, where the production and the consumption through individual or various free, comradely unions; whether the hand-craft or a similar system is not better suited to build up the personality than the extreme mechanization and rationalization; whether a single dwelling place is not more suitable than a dwelling-armory; whether the shortening of the work time doesn't depend more upon the quality of the product, or from the disposition of some superfluous things, than the surpassing of the mechanical mass production; whether no kind of education at all wouldn't be better than such an education that has as its aim the implanting within the mind of the child a Bolshevistic or fascistic mysticism; whether public activities, as child-protection, the care of motherhood, etc. could not just as well be created through mutual associations of the participants (for example, union for transport, for travel, for correspondence-relationship and so on), than through the State?

It can very calmly be asserted, that as much as there have disappeared the superstitions as to the inequality among races and sexes, it was but a result of the culture-height of the individual, and that there has been no need for any kind of interference from the State; that the freedom of custom is a question of personal ethics, an expression of the personal conception and has nothing to do with the guarantee of the State.

Thus, whereas the outspoken dictatorships or the masked ones declare before the entire world that force is the healing method for all the evils in society, we say, that only free-willingness can develop strong personalities.

Our ideas and conception of life, which we represent only for ourselves, deserves just as much consideration, as the idea and life conception of those who force their ideas upon others, without their consent. We declare, that where there exists a force-reign of society, there is no free choice and in that event, due to the education as well as to the administrative and policing organizations, the results will be a humanity, a society, an equality of slaves.

The Soviet Union could have a very simple method to receive the sympathies of the anarchists. It would have to, within its domain, give the anarchists an opportunity in an uninterfering way to experiment their ideas, that means to give them the liberty of expressing and propagandizing their views, to unite themselves and carry through their aims.

If the Soviet Union should accept this, it would mean giving the opportunity, for free competition, for free choice, But the body of authority lies in that of not allowing such an opportunity. A dictatorship does not want, that it should be chosen, that it should be compared with another regime, but has to be accepted. Whether one wants it or not. And one must not complain, nor speak out. There is no more despotic, oppressive system in the world.

There is no doubt that the economic as well as the for political mysticism of bolshevism and fascism there is marked the same fate as the Catholic mysticism. One nice day they will, as all former imperialistic formations, go down to perdition by the over measure of their dictatorship.

To the Friends of E. Armand

Friend, comrade:

It is now five years that our relations have been interrupted. And how much has happened since 1939! What has become of you? Will this communication reach you? Have you not had to seek refuge in a place quite distant from the locality where you received "l'en dehors"? Or perhaps you haven't changed address and have passed through the troubled period we lived through without too much damage. Who knows, perhaps you are somewhere in Germany a prisoner, a deportee? Whatever the case, with this letter we are attempting to tie back together the broken thread of our relations with you.

Perhaps you want news of me? After the banning of "l'en dehors," and following a short stay of three months in a hospitable cage, a stay due to the finding on my person a translation of a pacifist manifesto that wasn't to the taste of the leaders of the period, I found myself sent to various concentration camps. I left the last of them in 1941, thanks to the intervention of comrades in the proofreader's union. (In total ten wasted years vegetating in governmental jails. My time certainly could have been put to more profitable use.) As soon as I returned I strived, clandestinely and as far as was possible, to meet, especially in Paris, those of ours who were spared by the horrible torment. I succeeded in this up to a certain point.

I think that the publication of a

periodical like "l'en dehors" is premature. I will only cite a few reasons. The need for an authorization. The rarity of paper. The cost of printing. The rise in postal taxes. Much has changed in costs since 1939. Nevertheless, we intend to have appear, as soon as this is possible, a review, a bulletin or some other periodical message aimed at maintaining between us the ties of friendship and camaraderie that the passing of time was not able to shake.

For the moment I limit myself to once again giving life and activity to our periodic meetings in Paris. You will find attached the expose of the theses and tendencies of this Center which, until further notice, will meet the last Monday of the month, at 7:30 pm at the office where, before the war, the friends and readers of "l'e.d" met.

Nevertheless we would like to know if, in case we start publication of a periodical (we have already chosen as its title "L'Unique"), we can count on your subscription. This would be useful to us, since the number of subscribers to a periodical can help it obtain a lowering of its postal taxes. We aren't fixing the price of a subscription, since we don't yet know the format, the number of pages, the frequency and the cost of the projected publication. Below you will find a subscription coupon.

You will also find a donation coupon, a donation aimed a permitting us to gather together some funds in advance so as to not find ourselves in financial difficulties at the moment we start up the periodical in question, or any other work of propaganda. It goes without saying that this donation is absolutely independent of the subscription coupon.

In good camaraderie and friendship:

E. Armand

Principal Tendencies and Theses of the "L'Unique" Center

Individual culture and education

Life as will and responsibility

Violence (the ideology of domination, imposition, exploitation, etc) as the origin of wars.

Reciprocity as the ethic of sociability

While waiting for a world where suffering will have been reduced to a tiny minimum, its elimination from relations conditioned by friendship and camaraderie.

Fidelity to the word given and to the clauses of

pacts freely consented to, and this in all domains

Voluntary and contractual associationism, cooperatism, and mutualism in all branches of human activity.

Liberation from prejudices concerning race, external appearance, inequality of sexes and social conditions, etc.

Personal life as a work of art.

The non-interference in the sphere of activity of others determining the limits to the expansion of the personality.

Reasoned Eugenics and thought out naturism

Combat against prostitution in all its forms and against the idea of the woman considered solely as a "physiological necessity."

Sensitivity, the spirit of understanding and

reconciliation, the fight against the attitude of "too-bad-for-you" as facts of internal vitality.

Practice of "first clean up in front of your door" before getting involved in the affairs of others.

Interest in free circles, libertarian colonies, innovative schools.

Pluralism in friendship, exclusive of preferences and privileges.

In case of special attention in one particular direction, this latter will always be in favor of he who has suffered most because of the spreading or realization of one, another, or several of the above theses.

Individualist Perspectives

The anarchist individualists do not present themselves as proletarians, absorbed only in the search for material amelioration, tied to a class determined to transform the world and to substitute a new society for the actual one. They place themselves in the present; they disdain to orient the coming generations towards a form of society allegedly destined to assure their happiness, for the simple reason that from the individualist point of view happiness is a conquest, an individuals internal realization.

Even if I believed in the efficacy of a universal social transformation, according to a well-defined system, without direction, sanction, or obligation, I do not see by what right I could persuade others that it is the best. For example, I want to live in a society from which the last vestige of authority has disappeared, but, to speak frankly, I am not certain that the "mass," to call it what it is, is capable of dispensing with authority. I want to live in a society in which the members think by and for themselves, but the attraction which is exercised on the mass by publicity, the press, frivolous reading and by State-subsidized distractions is such that I ask myself whether men will ever be able to reflect and judge with an independent mind.

I may be told in reply that the solution of the social question will transform every man into a sage. This is a gratuitous affirmation, the more so as there have been sages under all regimes. Since I do not know the social form which is most likely to create internal harmony and equilibrium in social unity, I refrain from theorizing.

When "voluntary association" is spoken of, voluntary adhesion to a plan, a project, a given action, this implies the possibility of refusing the association, adhesion or action. Let us imagine the planet submitted to a single social or economic life; how would I exist if this system did not please me? There remains to me only one expedient: to integrate or to perish. It is held that, "the social question" having been solved, there is no longer a place for non-conformism, recalcitrance, etc..... but it is precisely when a question has been resolved that it is important to pose new ones or to return to an old solution, if only to avoid stagnation.

If there is a "Freedom" standing over and above all individuals, it is surely nothing more than the expression of their thoughts, the manifestation and diffusion of their opinions. The existence of a social organization founded on a single ideological unity interdicts all exercise of freedom of speech and of ideologically contrary thought. How would I be able to oppose the dominant system, proposing another, supporting a return to an older system, if the means of making my view-point known or of publicizing my critiques were in the possession of the agents of the regime in power? This regime must either accept reproach when compared to other social solutions superior to its own, or, despite its termination in "ist," it is no better than any other regime. Either it will admit opposition, secession, schism, fractionalism, competition, or nothing will distinguish it significantly from a dictatorship. This "ist" regime would undoubtedly claim that it has been invested with its power by the masses, that it does not exercise its power or control except by the delegation of assemblies or congresses; but as long as it did not allow the intransigents and refractories to express the reasons for their attitude and for their corresponding behaviour, it would be only a totalitarian system. The material benefits on which a dictatorship prides itself are of no importance. Regardless of whether there is scarcity or abundance, a dictatorship is always a dictatorship.

It is asked of me why I call my individualism "anarchist individualism"? Simply because the State concretizes the best organized form of resistance to individual affirmation. What is the State? An organism which bills itself as representative of the social body, to which power is allegedly delegated, this power expressing the will of an autocrat or of popular sovereignty. This power has no reason for existing other than the maintenance of the extant social structure. But individual aspirations are unable to come to term with the existence of the State, personification of Society, for, as Palante says: "All society is and will be exploitative, usurpacious, dominating, and tyrannical. This it is not by accident but by essence." Yet the individualist would be neither exploited, usurped, dominated, tyrannized nor dispossessed of his sovereignty. On the other hand, Society is able to exercise its constraint on the individual only thanks to the support of the State, administrator and director of the affairs of Society. No matter which way he turns the individual encounters the State or its agents of execution, who do not care in the least whether the regulations which they enforce concur or not with the diversity of temperaments of the subjects upon whom they are administered. From their aspirations as from their demands, the individualists of our school have eliminated the State. That is why they call themselves "anarchists."

But we deceive ourselves if we imagine that the individualists of our school are anarchists (AN-ARCHY, etymologically, mans only negation of the state, and does not pertain to other matters) only in relation to the State – such as the western democracies or the totalitarian systems. This point cannot be overemphasized. Against all that which is power, that is, economic as well as political domination, esthetic as well as intellectual, scientific as well as ethical, the individualists rebel and form such fronts as they are able, alone or in voluntary association. In effect, a group or federation can exercise power as absolute as any State if it accepts in a given field all the possibilities of activity and realization.

The only social body in which it is possible for an individualist to evolve and develop is that which admits a concurrent plurality of experiences and realizations, to which is opposed all groupings founded on an ideological exclusiveness, which, well-meant though they may be, threaten the integrity of the individual from the moment that this exclusiveness aims to extend itself to the non-adherents of the grouping. To call this anti-statist would be doing no more than provoking a mask for an appetite for driving a herd of human sheep.

I have said above that it is necessary to

insist on this point. For example, anarchist communism denies, rejects and expels the State from its ideology; but it resuscitates it the moment that it substitutes social organization for personal judgment. If anarchist individualism thus has in common with anarchist communism the political negation of the State, of the "Arche," it only marks a point of divergence. Anarchist communism places itself on the economic plane, on the terrain of the class struggle, united with syndicalism, etc. (this is its right), but anarchist individualism situates itself on the psychological plane, and on that of resistance to social totalitarianism, which is something entirely different. (Naturally, anarchist individualism follows the many paths of activity and education: philosophy, literature, ethics, etc., but I have wanted to make precise here only some points of our attitude to the social environment.)

I do not deny that this is not very new, but it is taking a position to which it is good to return from time to time.

www.ingramcontent.com/pod-product-compliance
Lightning Source LLC
Chambersburg PA
CBHW072111280526
45788CB00006B/2487